To:

....

From:

....

Date:

....

D1315333

101 Words that Matter Most for Women

© 2012 Christian Art Gifts, RSA
      Christian Art Gifts Inc., IL, USA

Designed by Christian Art Gifts

Images used under license from Shutterstock.com

Scripture quotations marked NIV are taken from the *Holy Bible*, New International Version® NIV®. Copyright © 1973, 1978, 1984, 2011 by International Bible Society. Used by permission of Zondervan Publishing House. All rights reserved.

Scripture quotations marked NLT are taken from the *Holy Bible*, New Living Translation®, second edition. Copyright © 1996, 2004, 2007 by Tyndale House Publishers, Inc., Carol Stream, Illinois 60188. All rights reserved.

Scripture quotations marked NKJV are taken from the *Holy Bible,* New King James Version. Copyright © 1979, 1980, 1982 by Thomas Nelson, Inc. Used by permission. All rights reserved.

Scripture quotations marked MSG are taken from THE MESSAGE. Copyright © by Eugene H. Peterson, 1993, 1994, 1995, 1996, 2000, 2001, 2002 by NavPress Publishing Group. Used by permission.

Printed in China

ISBN 978-1-4321-0165-7

15　16　17　18　19　20　21　22　23　24　–　15　14　13　12　11　10　9　8　7　6

101
Words that
Matter Most
for
Women

christian
art gifts®

Contents

Acceptance

ac·cept·ance /akˈseptəns/ *noun*

1. The act of accepting or the state of being accepted or acceptable. *2.* Favorable reception; approval. *3.* The state of being recognized or acknowledged. *4.* Affirmation, favor, recognition, seal of approval.

....

"If you do what is right, will you not be accepted? But if you do not do what is right, sin is crouching at your door; it desires to have you, but you must rule over it."
Gen. 4:7 NIV

"However, those the Father has given Me will come to Me, and I will never reject them."
John 6:37 NLT

Therefore, accept each other just as Christ has accepted you so that God will be given glory.
Rom. 15:7 NLT

....

Our entire confidence in our acceptance before God is based solely upon the fact that Jesus was our legal representative in His sinless life and obedient death.

- Jerry Bridges -

Appreciation

ap·pre·ci·a·tion/ə,priːʃiˈeɪʃn/***noun***

1. Thankfulness or gratitude for something someone has done for you. 2. The recognition and enjoyment of the good qualities of someone or something. 3. Acknowledgement, affection, commendation, esteem, gratitude, high regard, liking, love, respect, value.

···

Give thanks to the Lord, for He is good;
His love endures forever.
1 Chron. 16:34 NIV

Be thankful in all circumstances, for this is
God's will for you who belong to Christ Jesus.
1 Thess. 5:18 NLT

Enter into His gates with thanksgiving,
and into His courts with praise.
Be thankful to Him, and bless His name.
Ps. 100:4 NKJV

···

Our love for God and our appreciation of His love and forgiveness will be in proportion to the recognition of our sin and unworthiness.

- Dave Hunt -

Aspiration

as · pi · ra · tion /ˌæspəˈreɪʃn/ *noun*

1. **Strong desire, ambition, hope or longing to achieve something.** *2.* **Steadfast longing for a higher goal, earnest desire for something.** *3.* **Aim, dream, eagerness, endeavor, longing, objective, passion, pursuit, urge, yearning.**

....

The aspirations of good people end in celebration.
Prov. 10:28 MSG

I press on toward the goal to win the prize for which God has called me.
Phil. 3:14 NIV

Aspire to lead a quiet life, to mind your own business, and to work with your own hands.
1 Thess. 4:11 NKJV

....

Your aspirations are your possibilities.
- Samuel Johnson -

Assurance

as·sur·ance /əˈʃʊrəns/ *noun*

1. Confidence or certainty in one's own abilities. **2.** A positive declaration intended to inspire confidence or give encouragement. **3.** A promise or pledge of support. **4.** Affirmation, guarantee, promise, security, vow, word of honor, conviction, courage, faith, sureness, trust.

....

Let us draw near to God with a sincere heart and with the full assurance that faith brings.
Heb. 10:22 NIV

For we know that if our earthly house, this tent, is destroyed, we have a building from God, a house not made with hands, eternal in the heavens.
2 Cor. 5:1 NKJV

The work of righteousness will be peace, and the effect of righteousness, quietness and assurance forever.
Isa. 32:17 NKJV

....

In the darkest of nights cling to the assurance that God loves you, that He always has advice for you, a path that you can tread and a solution to your problem. God never disappoints anyone who places his trust in Him.

- Basilea Schlink -

Attitude

at · ti · tude/'ætɪtuːd/*noun*

1. **A complex mental state involving beliefs, feelings, values and dispositions to act in certain ways.** *2.* **The way a person views something or tends to behave towards it.** *3.* **Character, frame of mind, mindset, outlook, perspective, stance, temperament.**

....

*May the God who gives endurance
and encouragement give you the same attitude
of mind toward each other that Christ Jesus had.*
Rom. 15:5 NIV

Be tenderhearted, and keep a humble attitude.
1 Pet. 3:8 NLT

*Let the Spirit renew your thoughts and attitudes.
Put on your new nature, created to be
like God – truly righteous and holy.*
Eph. 4:23-24 NLT

....

Wherever you go, no matter what the weather,
always bring your own sunshine.

- *Anthony J. D'Angelo* -

Balance

bal · ance /ˈbaləns/ *noun*

1. Equipoise between contrasting, opposing, or interacting elements. *2.* Achieving harmony between main areas of life: God, family, work, self. *3.* Equilibrium, stability, judgment.

....

God, give me just enough to satisfy my needs.
Prov. 30:8 NLT

Whatever your hand finds to do,
do it with all your might.
Eccles. 9:10 NIV

Be joyful. Grow to maturity.
Encourage each other.
Live in harmony and peace.
Then the God of love and peace will be with you.
2 Cor. 13:11 NLT

....

Happiness is not a matter of intensity but of balance and order and rhythm and harmony.

- Thomas Merton -

Beauty

beau · ty /ˈbjuːti/ ***noun***

1. **A particularly graceful, ornamental, or excellent quality. 2. The quality present in a person that gives intense pleasure or deep satisfaction to the mind, including a personality in which high spiritual qualities are manifest. 3. Attractiveness, loveliness, magnificence, splendor.**

....

Charm is deceptive, and beauty does not last;
but a woman who fears the Lord will be greatly praised.
Prov. 31:30 NLT

You should be known for the beauty that
comes from within, the unfading beauty of a
gentle and quiet spirit, which is so precious to God.
1 Pet. 3:4 NLT

People judge by outward appearance,
but the Lord looks at the heart.
1 Sam. 16:7 NLT

....

Characteristics which define beauty
are wholeness, harmony and radiance.

- Thomas Aquinas -

Bible

bi · ble/ˈbībəl/***noun***

1. A divinely inspired Book consisting of 66 books written by various authors and divided into the Old and New Testaments. 2. Contains the message of salvation for all people and is a guidebook for Christians on how to live. 3. Good News, Holy Scriptures, Word of God.

....

Your word is a lamp to my feet and a light to my path.
Ps. 119:105 NKJV

The word of God is alive and active.
Sharper than any double-edged sword.
Heb. 4:12 NIV

All Scripture is inspired by God and is useful
to teach us what is true and to make us realize
what is wrong in our lives. It corrects us when
we are wrong and teaches us to do what is right.
2 Tim. 3:16 NLT

....

The Bible is to me the most precious thing in the
world just because it tells me the story of Jesus.

– George MacDonald –

Career

ca·reer/kəˈrɪr/*noun*

1. An occupation undertaken for a significant period of a person's life, usually with opportunities for progress. *2.* Calling, life work, pursuit, vocation.

....

Work willingly at whatever you do, as though you were working for the Lord rather than for people.
Col. 3:23 NLT

Always give yourself fully to the work of the Lord, because you know that your labor in the Lord is not in vain.
1 Cor. 15:58 NIV

Make a careful exploration of who you are and the work you have been given, and then sink yourself into that. Don't be impressed with yourself. Don't compare yourself with others. Each of you must take responsibility for doing the creative best you can with your own life.
Gal. 6:4 MSG

....

He who loves his work never labors.
- *Jim Stovell* -

Challenges

chal·lenges /'tʃælɪndʒ/ *noun*

1. A demanding or stimulating task or situation.
2. Dare, test, threat, trial.

....

Consider it a sheer gift when tests and challenges come at you from all sides. You know that under pressure, your faith-life is forced into the open and shows its true colors.
James 1:4 MSG

In quietness and confidence is your strength.
Isa. 30:15 NLT

Examine me, O Lord, and prove me;
try my mind and my heart.
Ps. 26:2 NKJV

....

In order to get from what was to what will be,
you must go through what is.

– *Anonymous* –

Character

char·ac·ter/kærəktər/*noun*

1. The combination of traits and qualities distinctive to an individual. **2.** Moral force, integrity, good reputation. **3.** Honor, individuality, strength, uprightness.

....

Choose a good reputation over great riches;
being held in high esteem is better than silver or gold.
Prov. 22:1 NLT

When the Lord comes, He will bring to
light what is hidden in darkness and
will expose the motives of the heart.
At that time each will receive their praise from God.
1 Cor. 4:5 NIV

"You're blessed when you get your inside
world – your mind and heart – put right.
Then you can see God in the outside world."
Matt. 5:8 MSG

....

Character is what you are in the dark.
- Dwight L. Moody -

Church

church /tʃɜːrtʃ/ *noun*

1. The body of believers who gather together to worship, pray and learn from God's Word.
2. Community, congregation, fellowship, sanctuary.

....

*Let us aim for harmony in the church
and try to build each other up.*
Rom. 14:19 NLT

*Everything must be done so that
the church may be built up.*
1 Cor. 14:26 NIV

*The house of God is the church of the living God,
the pillar and ground of the truth.*
1 Tim. 3:15 NKJV

....

Now the church is not of wood and stone, but
the company of people who believe in Christ.

- *Martin Luther* -

Comfort

com · fort/ˈkʌmfərt/*noun*

1. Consolation or relief from affliction, grief or anxiety. *2.* A person or thing that gives such consolation. *3.* Encourage, gladden, hearten, reassure, relieve, soothe.

....

You, O Lord, help and comfort me.
Ps. 86:17 NLT

"Do not be afraid or discouraged, for the Lord will personally go ahead of you. He will be with you; He will neither fail you nor abandon you."
Deut. 31:8 NLT

"As a mother comforts her child, so will I comfort you."
Isa. 66:13 NIV

....

In Christ the heart of the Father is revealed, and higher comfort there cannot be than to rest in the Father's heart.

– Andrew Murray –

Commitment

com · mit · ment /kəˈmɪtmənt/ ***noun***

1. The state or quality of being dedicated to a cause, action or attitude e.g. a committed Christian. *2.* Adherence, dedication, devotion, involvement, loyalty.

....

Give yourselves completely to God, for you were dead, but now you have new life. So use your whole body as an instrument to do what is right for the glory of God.
Rom. 6:13 NLT

Commit everything you do to the Lord. Trust Him, and He will help you.
Ps. 37:5 NLT

Let us not grow weary while doing good, for in due season we shall reap if we do not lose heart.
Gal. 6:9 NKJV

....

Give your all to Christ, who gave His all for you.

– *Anonymous* –

Compassion

com · pas · sion kəm'pæʃn/*noun*

1. A feeling of distress or pity for the suffering and misfortune of another, often including the desire to alleviate it. 2. Condolence, fellow feeling, heart, humanity, kindness, mercy.

....

You must be compassionate,
just as your Father is compassionate.
Luke 6:36 NLT

The Lord is good to everyone.
He showers compassion on all His creation.
Ps. 145:9 NLT

Return to the Lord your God, for He is gracious and
compassionate, slow to anger and abounding in love.
Joel 2:13 NIV

....

Compassion is to feel what it is like to live
inside someone else's skin. It is the knowledge
that there can never really be any peace and joy for
me until there is peace and joy finally for you too.

- Frederick Buechner -

Confidence

con · fi · dence /ˈkɑːnfɪdəns/ *noun*

1. The belief that one can have faith in or rely on someone or something. *2.* The state or quality of being certain. *3.* Belief, dependence, faith, reliance, trust.

....

I can do everything through Christ,
who gives me strength.
Phil. 4:13 NLT

You have been my hope, Sovereign Lord,
my confidence since my youth.
Ps. 71:5 NIV

"Blessed are those who trust in the Lord and have
made the Lord their hope and confidence."
Jer. 17:7 NLT

....

Faith is the deliberate confidence in
the character of God whose ways you
may not understand at the time.

- Oswald Chambers -

Contentment

con · tent · ment/kən'tentmənt/*noun*

**1. In a state of peaceful happiness or satisfaction.
2. Mentally or emotionally satisfied with things
as they are. 3. Comfort, ease, peace of mind,
willing to accept.**

....

*I have learned the secret of being content in
any and every situation, whether well fed or hungry,
whether living in plenty or in want. I can do all
this through Him who gives me strength.*
Phil. 4:12-13 NIV

*You will keep in perfect peace those whose
minds are steadfast, because they trust in You.*
Isa. 26:3 NIV

*Let your conduct be without covetousness;
be content with such things as you have. For He Himself
has said, "I will never leave you nor forsake you."*
Heb. 13:5 NKJV

....

Contentment is a distinguishing trait of a godly
person because he has his heart focused on God
rather than on possessions or positions of power.

– *Jerry Bridges* –

Courage

cour · age /ˈkɜːrɪdʒ/ **noun**

1. The power or quality of dealing with or facing danger, fear or pain. *2.* The courage of one's convictions: the confidence to act in accordance with one's beliefs. *3.* Boldness, bravery, firmness, grit.

......

"Be strong and courageous! Do not be afraid or discouraged. For the Lord your God is with you wherever you go."
Josh. 1:9 NLT

Watch, stand fast in the faith, be brave, be strong.
1 Cor. 16:13 NKJV

Wait on the Lord; be of good courage, and He shall strengthen your heart; wait, I say, on the Lord!
Ps. 27:14 NKJV

......

Keep your fears to yourself,
but share your courage with others.
- *Robert L. Stevenson* -

Decisions

de·ci·sions/dɪˈsɪʒns/*noun*

1. **A judgment, conclusion or resolution reached after consideration 2. The quality of being decisive. 3. Determination, firmness of purpose, resoluteness, strength of mind.**

....

Show me the right path, O Lord;
point out the road for me to follow.
Ps. 25:4 NLT

Trust in the Lord with all your heart; do not
depend on your own understanding. Seek His will
in all you do and He will show you which path to take.
Prov. 3:5-6 NLT

Wise choices will watch over you.
Understanding will keep you safe.
Prov. 2:11 NLT

....

As we trust God to give us wisdom for today's decisions, He will lead us a step at a time into what He wants us to be doing in the future.

- *Theodore Epp* -

Dignity

dig · ni · ty/ˈdɪgnəti/*noun*

....

***1.** The state or quality of being worthy of honor or respect. **2.** Character, distinction, respectability, virtue, worth.*

....

Treat everyone you meet with dignity.
1 Pet. 2:17 MSG

Remember that your bodies are created with the same dignity as the Master's body.
1 Cor. 6:15 MSG

Love each other with genuine affection, and take delight in honoring each other.
Rom. 12:10 NLT

....

There is a healthful hardiness about real dignity that never dreads contact and communion with others, however humble.

- *Washington Irving* -

Diligence

dil·i·gence/ˈdɪlɪdʒəns/***noun***

1. Careful and persistent work or effort.
2. Conscientious, hard-working, industrious, persevering, persistent.

....

The diligent find freedom in their work;
the lazy are oppressed by work.
Prov. 12:24 MSG

Watch out that you do not lose what
we have worked so hard to achieve.
Be diligent so that you receive your full reward.
2 John 1:8 NLT

Committed and persistent work pays off.
Prov. 28:20 MSG

....

Let's be diligent in giving, careful
in our living and faithful in our praying.

- Jack Hyles -

Discernment

dis · cern · ment /dɪ'sɜːrnmənt/ *noun*

1. **Keen perception or judgment. Clear-sighted, discriminating, intelligent, perceptive, sensitive, wise.**

....

If you need wisdom, ask our generous God, and He will give it to you. He will not rebuke you for asking.
James 1:5 NLT

Fear of the Lord is the beginning of knowledge.
Prov. 1:7 NKJV

The heart of the discerning acquires knowledge, for the ears of the wise seek it out.
Prov. 18:15 NIV

....

Discernment is not simply telling the difference between right and wrong, rather it is telling the difference between right and almost right.

– *Charles H. Spurgeon* –

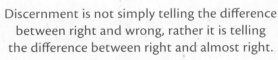

Dreams

dreams/driːm/*noun*

1. **A cherished ambition, hope, aspiration or ideal.**

....

Take delight in the Lord, and He
will give you your heart's desires.
Ps. 37:4 NLT

God can do anything, you know –
far more than you could ever imagine or
guess or request in your wildest dreams!
Eph. 3:20 MSG

Cheerfully pleasing God is the main thing,
and that's what we aim to do.
2 Cor. 5:9 MSG

....

You are never too old to set a new
goal or to dream a new dream.

- C. S. Lewis -

Empowerment

em · pow · er · ment /ɪmˈpaʊərmənt/ *noun*

1. **Give authority, confidence, power or strength to. 2. Allow, enable, entitle, qualify, warrant.**

....

"Not by might nor by power,
but by My Spirit," says the Lord Almighty.
Zech. 4:6 NIV

"But the Advocate, the Holy Spirit, whom the Father
will send in My name, will teach you all things and
will remind you of everything I have said to you."
John 14:26 NIV

God's Way is not a matter of mere talk;
it's an empowered life.
1 Cor. 4:18 MSG

....

The Holy Spirit is the gift of the Risen Christ.
His anointing, filling, empowering work is
a baptism of love that gives power to make
Jesus real to you and known to others.

- Winkie Pratney -

Encouragement

en · cour · age · ment /ɪnˈkɜːrɪdʒmənt/ *noun*

1. To inspire (someone) with the courage or confidence (to do something). **2.** Comfort, boost, help, inspirit, reassure, support.

....

Let all who seek God's help be encouraged.
Ps. 69:32 NLT

If your gift is to encourage others, be encouraging.
Rom. 12:8 NLT

Such things were written in the Scriptures long ago to teach us. And the Scriptures give us hope and encouragement as we wait patiently for God's promises to be fulfilled.
Rom. 15:4 NLT

....

A smile of encouragement at the right moment may act like sunlight on a closed up flower; it may be the turning point for a struggling life.

– Alfred Montapert –

Energy

en·er·gy/ˈenərdʒi/*noun*

1. The strength and vitality required for
sustained activity. **2.** Exertion, intensity,
stamina, strength, strenuousness.

....

*Those who wait on the Lord shall renew their strength;
they shall mount up with wings like eagles, they shall
run and not be weary, they shall walk and not faint.*
Isa. 40:31 NKJV

*"Come to Me, all you who are weary
and burdened, and I will give you rest."*
Matt. 11:28 NIV

*Let yourselves be pulled into a way of life shaped
by God's life, a life energetic and blazing with holiness.*
1 Pet. 1:15 MSG

....

After spending time alone with God, we find that He
injects into our bodies energy, power and strength.

- Charles Stanley -

Enthusiasm

en·thu·si·asm /ɪn'θuːziæzəm/ *noun*

1. Intense enjoyment, interest or approval.
2. Ardent and lively interest or eagerness.
3. Devotion, excitement, passion, warmth,
zeal, zest.

....

Work hard and serve the Lord enthusiastically.
Rom. 12:11 NLT

*Always work enthusiastically for the Lord, for you
know that nothing you do for the Lord is ever useless.*
1 Cor. 15:58 NLT

*Bravo, bravissimo! Shout God-songs at the
top of your lungs! Sing songs to God, sing out!
Sing to our King, sing praise! He's Lord
over earth, so sing your best songs to God.*
Ps. 47:1-7 MSG

....

People rarely succeed unless they
have fun in what they are doing.

- *Dale Carnegie* -

Eternity

e · ter · ni · ty /ɪˈtɜːrnəti/ *noun*

1. Infinite or unending time. **2.** Endless life after death. **3.** The time a Christian will spend in the presence of Father God and Jesus Christ, Savior and Redeemer of mankind. **4.** Endlessness, forever, heaven, immortality.

....

"In My Father's house are many mansions; if it were not so, I would have told you. I go to prepare a place for you."
John 14:2 NKJV

"I tell you the truth, anyone who believes has eternal life."
John 6:47 NLT

"He who believes in the Son has everlasting life."
John 3:36 NKJV

....

If you read history you will find that the Christians who did most for the present world were precisely those who thought most of the next.

- *C. S. Lewis* -

Faith

faith/feɪθ/*noun*

1. Complete trust or confidence in someone or something. *2.* Strong, unshakable belief in God and His actions and promises. *3.* Assurance, certainty, conviction, reliance, security.

....

The fundamental fact of existence is that this trust in God, this faith, is the firm foundation under everything that makes life worth living.
Heb. 11:1 MSG

Fight the good fight of faith, lay hold on eternal life, to which you were also called.
1 Tim. 6:12 NKJV

"All things are possible to him who believes."
Mark 9:23 NKJV

....

God always gives His best to those
who leave the choice with Him.

– *Jim Elliot* –

Faithfulness

faith · ful · ness /ˈfeɪθflnəs/ *noun*

1. The quality of a loyal and steadfast follower of Christ and a divine quality of our loyal and loving God. *2.* Devoted, reliable, resolute, true, steadfast, staunch, unwavering.

·····················

*Thank You for Your love, thank You for
Your faithfulness; most holy is Your name,
most holy is Your Word. The moment I called out,
You stepped in; You made my life large with strength.*
Ps. 138:2-3 MSG

*Because of the Lord's great love we are not
consumed, for His compassions never fail. They
are new every morning; great is Your faithfulness.*
Lam. 3:22-23 NIV

*Your love, Lord, reaches to the heavens,
Your faithfulness to the skies.*
Ps. 36:5 NIV

·····················

Our need is not to prove God's
faithfulness but to demonstrate our own,
by trusting Him both to determine and to
supply our needs according to His will.

– John MacArthur –

Family

fam · i · ly /'fæməli/ *noun*

1. All the persons living together in one household. 2. An association of people who share common beliefs or activities. 3. Community, fellowship, home, unit.

....

God decided in advance to adopt us into His own family by bringing us to Himself through Jesus Christ.
Eph. 1:5 NLT

What marvelous love the Father has extended to us! Just look at it – we're called children of God! That's who we really are.
1 John 3:1 MSG

Her children arise and call her blessed; her husband also, and he praises her: "Many women do noble things, but you surpass them all."
Prov. 31:28-29 NIV

....

A family is a place where principles are hammered and honed on the anvil of everyday living.

- Chuck Swindoll -

Fellowship

fel · low · ship/ˈfeloʊʃɪp/*noun*

1. The state of sharing mutual beliefs, interests, experiences, activities. *2.* Mutual trust and charitableness between Christians. *3.* Communion, companionship, friendship, *koinonia*, relationship, sisterhood.

....

How good and pleasant it is when
God's people live together in unity!
Ps. 133:1 NIV

In Christ we, though many, form one body,
and each member belongs to all the others.
Rom. 12:5 NIV

If we walk in the light as He is in the light,
we have fellowship with one another, and the
blood of Jesus Christ His Son cleanses us from all sin.
1 John 1:7 NKJV

....

Our love for God is measured by our everyday
fellowship with others and the love it displays.

– Andrew Murray –

Finances

fi · nanc · es/ˈfaɪnænses/*noun*

1. The money available to a person and the way this money is managed. 2. Assets, cash in hand, funds, monetary resources.

....

Keep your lives free from the love of money and be content with what you have.
Heb. 13:5 NIV

You can be sure that God will take care of everything you need, His generosity exceeding even yours in the glory that pours from Jesus.
Phil. 4:19 MSG

[Don't] be so preoccupied with getting, so you can respond to God's giving. Steep your life in God-reality, God-initiative, God-provisions. Don't worry about missing out. You'll find all your everyday human concerns will be met.
Matt. 6:33 MSG

....

Money is not required to buy
one necessity of the soul.

- Henry David Thoreau -

Forgiveness

for · give · ness /fər'givnis/ ***noun***

1. The act of forgiving or the state of being forgiven by God. **2.** Willingness to forgive. **3.** Absolution, mercy, pardon, remission.

....

Make allowance for each other's faults,
and forgive anyone who offends you. Remember,
the Lord forgave you, so you must forgive others.
Col. 3:13 NLT

If we confess our sins to Him, He is faithful and just to
forgive us our sins and to cleanse us from all wickedness.
1 John 1:9 NLT

As far as the east is from the west,
so far has He removed our transgressions from us.
Ps. 103:12 NKJV

....

God pardons like a mother who kisses
away the repentant tears of her child.

- Henry Ward Beecher -

Freedom

free · dom /'friːdəm/ *noun*

1. The ability to move without constraint in the sphere for which God made us, it is not the right and ability to do as one pleases. **2.** The condition of being free from the constraints and condition of sin through Jesus Christ and His death on the Cross.

....

When we died with Christ we
were set free from the power of sin.
Rom. 6:7 NLT

Christ has set us free to live a new life.
So take your stand!
Gal. 5:1 MSG

You are free, yet you are God's slaves,
so don't use your freedom as an excuse to do evil.
1 Pet. 2:16 NLT

....

God's purpose in redeeming men from sin is not to give them freedom to do as they please but freedom to do as He pleases, which is to live righteously.

- *John MacArthur* -

Friendship

friend · ship/'frendʃɪp/*noun*

1. Relationship between two or more people who are well known to one another and regarded with liking, affection and loyalty. *2.* Bond, companionship, confidante, intimacy, familiarity.

· ·

A friend is always loyal.
Prov. 17:17 NLT

Two are better than one, because they
have a good return for their labor.
Eccles. 4:9 NIV

We can rejoice in our wonderful
new relationship with God because our
Lord Jesus Christ has made us friends of God.
Rom. 5:11 NLT

· ·

Friendship is born at that moment when
one person says to another: What! You too?
I thought I was the only one.

– *C. S. Lewis* –

Fulfillment

ful · fill · ment /fʊlˈfɪlmənt/ *noun*

1. To do or achieve what was hoped for or expected. *2.* To achieve one's potential or desires. *3.* Contentment, delight, gratification, happiness, pleasure, satisfaction.

....

He satisfies the thirsty and fills the hungry with good things.
Ps. 107:9 NLT

You will keep in perfect peace all who trust in You, all whose thoughts are fixed on You!
Isa. 26:3 NLT

Because I am righteous, I will see You. When I awake, I will see You face to face and be satisfied.
Ps. 17:15 NLT

....

Your greatest fulfillment in life will come when you discover your unique gifts and abilities and use them to edify others and glorify the Lord.

– Neil T. Anderson –

Future

fu · ture/ˈfjuːtʃər/*noun*

1. The time yet to come. **2.** Undetermined events that will occur in that time. **3.** By-and-by, hereafter, time from now on, tomorrow.

....

"I know the plans I have for you," says the Lord.
"They are plans for good and not for disaster,
to give you a future and a hope."
Jer. 29:11 NLT

The Lord will work out His plans for my life.
Ps. 138:8 NLT

There is surely a future hope for you,
and your hope will not be cut off.
Prov. 23:18 NIV

....

The future is as bright as the promises of God.

– Adoniram Judson –

Generosity

gen·er·os·i·ty/ˌdʒenəˈrɑːsəti/*noun*

1. Willingness and liberality in giving away one's money, gifts, kindness, time. 2. Freedom from pettiness in character and mind. 3. A generous act 4. Big-hearted, bountiful, hospitable, lavish, unstinting.

....

I am praying that you will put into action the generosity that comes from your faith as you understand and experience all the good things we have in Christ.
Philem. 1:6 NLT

You know the generous grace of our Lord Jesus Christ. Though He was rich, yet for your sakes He became poor, so that by His poverty He could make you rich.
2 Cor. 8:9 NLT

He who sows sparingly will also reap sparingly, and he who sows bountifully will also reap bountifully.
2 Cor. 9:6 NKJV

....

He, who gives what He would as readily throw away, gives without generosity; for the essence of generosity is in self-sacrifice.

- *Jeremy Taylor* -

Gifts

gifts/gɪft/*noun*

1. **Something given.** *2.* **A special aptitude, ability, or power; talent.** *3.* **Bestowed on Christians by the Holy Spirit to strengthen the church.**

···

In His grace, God has given us different gifts for doing certain things well.
Rom. 12:6 NLT

What happens when we live God's way? He brings gifts into our lives, much the same way that fruit appears in an orchard – things like affection for others, exuberance about life, serenity.
Gal. 5:22 MSG

To those who use well what they are given, even more will be given, and they will have an abundance.
Matt. 25:29 NLT

···

Our purpose should be to discover the gifts He has given us and to use those gifts faithfully and joyfully in His service, without either envying or disparaging the gifts we do not have.

– John MacArthur –

God

God /gɑːd/ *noun*

1. The sole Supreme Being, eternal, spiritual, transcendent, who is the Creator and ruler of the universe and is infinite in all attributes
2. The Almighty, Our Father, the Omnipresent, the Omnipotent, the Omniscient, the All-Merciful.

....

*In the beginning God created
the heavens and the earth.*
Gen. 1:1 NIV

*For God so loved the world that He gave
His one and only Son, that whoever believes
in Him shall not perish but have eternal life.*
John 3:16 NIV

"Our Father in heaven, hallowed be Your name."
Matt. 6:9 NKJV

....

God dwells in His creation and is everywhere
indivisibly present in all His works.

- A. W. Tozer -

Godliness

god · li · ness /'gɑːdliness/ *noun*

1. Having a great reverence for God and attempting to live a holy life that is pleasing to God. **2.** Christlike, devout, faithful, God-loving, God-fearing, pure in heart, righteous.

....

Godliness with contentment is great gain.
1 Tim. 6:6 NIV

Pursue righteousness, godliness, faith, love, endurance and gentleness.
1 Tim. 6:11 NIV

These are the wholesome teachings of the Lord Jesus Christ. These teachings promote a godly life.
1 Tim. 6:3 NLT

....

Prayer – secret, fervent, believing prayer –
lies at the root of all personal godliness.

- William Carey -

Goodness

good · ness/ˈɡʊdnəs/*noun*

1. The state or quality of being good.
2. Generosity. **3.** Honor, integrity, kindness,
moral excellence, virtue.

....

*Make every effort to add to your
faith goodness; and to goodness, knowledge.*
2 Pet. 1:5 NIV

*The fruit of the Spirit is love, joy,
peace, forbearance, kindness, goodness,
faithfulness, gentleness and self-control.*
Gal. 5:22-23 NIV

*"A good person produces good deeds
and words season after season."*
Matt. 12:35 MSG

....

The supreme test of goodness is not
in the greater but in the smaller
incidents of our character and practice.

– F. B. Meyer –

Grace

grace/ɡreɪs/*noun*

1. The free and unmerited favor of God shown towards people. *2.* God's unmerited, undeserved gifts. *3.* Divine goodness, God's favor, God's love, mercy.

....

The Lord God gives us grace and glory.
He will withhold no good thing
from those who do what is right.
Ps. 84:11 NLT

God saved you by His grace when you believed.
It is a gift from God. Salvation is not a reward for the
good things we have done, so none of us can boast about it.
Eph. 2:8-9 NLT

Let us therefore come boldly to the throne
of grace, that we may obtain mercy
and find grace to help in time of need.
Heb. 4:16 NKJV

....

Grace, then, is grace – that is to say,
it is sovereign, it is free, it is sure,
it is unconditional, and it is everlasting.

- Alexander Whyte -

Gratitude

grat·i·tude/ˈɡrætɪtuːd/*noun*

1. The state of being grateful; thankfulness.
2. The feeling of being thankful and wanting
to express your thanks. **3.** Acknowledgement,
appreciation, recognition, thanksgiving.

....

*Thank God! Call out His Name! Tell the
whole world who He is and what He's done!*
1 Chron. 16:8 MSG

*Be cheerful no matter what; pray all the time;
thank God no matter what happens. This is the
way God wants you who belong to Christ Jesus to live.*
1 Thess. 5:18 MSG

*May you be filled with joy, always thanking the Father.
He has enabled you to share in the inheritance
that belongs to His people, who live in the light.*
Col. 1:11-12 NLT

....

Gratitude is the fairest blossom
which springs from the soul.

- Henry Ward Beecher -

Growth

growth/groʊθ/*noun*

1. The process of developing or maturing physically, mentally, or spiritually. **2.** Maturing from spiritual babes fed on milk to being able to digest the solid teachings of the Word. **3.** Advancement, development, improvement, maturity.

....

Let your roots grow down into Him,
and let your lives be built on Him.
Then your faith will grow strong in
the truth you were taught, and you
will overflow with thankfulness.
Col. 2:7 NLT

God who started this great work in you
will keep at it and bring it to a flourishing
finish on the very day Christ Jesus appears.
Phil. 1:6 MSG

Grow in the grace and knowledge of our Lord and Savior
Jesus Christ. To Him be glory both now and forever!
2 Pet. 3:18 NIV

....

Becoming like Christ is a long,
slow process of growth.

– *Rick Warren* –

Guidance

guid · ance/ˈɡaɪdns/*noun*

....

1. The act or process of guiding. **2.** God's direction and leading. **3.** Advice, council, enlightenment, help.

....

The Lord says, "I will guide you along the best pathway for your life. I will advise you and watch over you."
Ps. 32:8 NLT

God, teach me lessons for living so I can stay the course. Give me insight so I can do what You tell me – my whole life one long, obedient response.
Ps. 119:33 MSG

I will bless the Lord who guides me; even at night my heart instructs me.
Ps. 16:7 NLT

....

We learn about guidance primarily by learning about the Guide. It is the knowledge of God and His ways with men which ultimately gives us stability in doing His will.

- Sinclair B. Ferguson -

Holiness

ho · li · ness /ˈhoʊlinəs/ *noun*

1. The state or quality of being holy. 2. To be wholly dedicated and devoted to God, distinct and separate from the world's way of living. 3. Christlike, pure, righteous, saintly.

....

You must be holy in everything you do,
just as God who chose you is holy.
1 Pet. 1:15 NLT

Do not conform to the pattern of this world,
but be transformed by the renewing of your mind.
Then you will be able to test and approve what
God's will is – His good, pleasing and perfect will.
Rom. 12:2 NIV

Christ made us right with God; He made us
pure and holy, and He freed us from sin.
1 Cor. 1:30 NLT

....

If you think you can walk in holiness
without keeping up perpetual fellowship
with Christ, you have made a great mistake.
If you would be holy, you must live close to Jesus.

- Charles H. Spurgeon -

Honesty

hon · es · ty/ˈɑːnəsti /*noun*

1. **The quality or fact of being honest
and truthful; uprightness and fairness.**
2. **Trustworthiness, sincerity, or frankness.**
3. **Freedom from deceit or fraud.**

....

*I know, my God, that You examine our
hearts and rejoice when You find integrity there.*
1 Chron. 29:17 NLT

*Honesty lives confident and carefree,
but Shifty is sure to be exposed.*
Prov. 10:9 MSG

*Truthful words stand the test of time,
but lies are soon exposed.*
Prov. 12:19 NLT

....

A half truth is a whole lie.
- Yiddish Proverb -

Honor

hon·or/ˈɑːnər/*noun*

1. To hold in great respect, esteem, or an outward sign of this. **2.** To worship. **3.** Exalt, glorify, praise, revere, venerate.

....

Now to the King eternal, immortal, invisible, to God who alone is wise, be honor and glory forever and ever. Amen.
1 Tim. 1:17 NKJV

"You are worthy, our Lord and God, to receive glory and honor and power, for You created all things, and by Your will they were created and have their being."
Rev. 4:11 NIV

"I will honor those who honor Me, and I will despise those who think lightly of Me."
1 Sam. 2:30 NLT

....

Every Christian bears Christ's name;
live as an honor to His name.

– Woodrow Kroll –

Hope

hope /hoʊp/ *noun*

1. A feeling of desire for something and confidence in the possibility of its fulfillment. 2. A person or thing that gives cause for hope. 3. To trust, believe. 4. Assurance, conviction, expectation, faith, reliance.

....

The fundamental fact of existence is that this trust in God, this faith, is the firm foundation under everything that makes life worth living. It's our handle on what we can't see.
Heb. 11:1 MSG

Lord, You alone are my hope.
I've trusted You, O Lord, from childhood.
Ps. 71:5 NLT

Those who hope in the Lord will renew their strength. They will soar on wings like eagles; they will run and not grow weary, they will walk and not be faint.
Isa. 40:31 NIV

....

Jesus gives us hope because He keeps us company, has a vision and knows the way we should go.

- Max Lucado -

Hospitality

hos · pi · tal · i · ty /ˌhɑːspɪˈtæləti/ **noun**

1. The friendly and generous reception and entertainment of guests, visitors, or strangers.
2. Amicable, cordial, genial, gracious, warm, welcoming, open-handed.

....

*Cheerfully share your home with those
who need a meal or a place to stay.*
1 Pet. 4:9 NLT

*Be ready with a meal or a bed when
it's needed. Why, some have extended
hospitality to angels without ever knowing it!*
Heb. 13:2 MSG

*What I'm interested in seeing you do is: sharing your
food with the hungry, inviting the homeless poor into
your homes, putting clothes on the shivering ill-clad.*
Isa. 58:7 MSG

....

The ornaments of your house will
be the guests who frequent it.

– *Anonymous* –

Humility

hu · mil · i · ty /hjuːˈmɪləti/ *noun*

1. **A modest or low view of one's own importance; humbleness. 2. The state or quality of being humble. 3. Lack of pride, modesty, unpretentiousness.**

....

God opposes the proud but favors the humble.
James 4:6 NLT

Always be humble and gentle. Be patient
with each other, making allowance
for each other's faults because of your love.
Eph. 4:2 NLT

You save the humble but bring low
those whose eyes are haughty.
Ps. 18:27 NIV

....

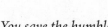

Pride builds walls between people,
humility builds bridges.

– *Rick Warren* –

Integrity

in · teg · ri · ty /ɪnˈtɛgrəti/ *noun*

1. The quality of being honest and having strong moral principles; moral uprightness.
2. Character, decency, principle, purity, virtue.

....

He who walks with integrity walks securely.
Prov. 10:9 NKJV

"Blessed are the pure in heart, for they shall see God."
Matt. 5:8 NKJV

This is what He requires of you: to do what is right, to love mercy, and to walk humbly with your God.
Mic. 6:8 NLT

....

Confidence on the outside begins
by living with integrity on the inside.

– *Anonymous* –

Joy

joy /jdʒɔɪ/ *noun*

1. A deep feeling or condition of happiness or contentment *2.* Something causing such a feeling; a source of happiness. *3.* An outward show of pleasure or delight; rejoicing. *4.* Contentment, gladness, pleasure, satisfaction.

·····················

The joy of God is your strength!
Neh. 8:10 MSG

The Lord helps me and my heart is filled with joy.
Ps. 28:7 NLT

Satisfy us in the morning with Your unfailing love,
that we may sing for joy and be glad all our days.
Ps. 90:14 NIV

·····················

True joy comes only from God and He shares this joy with those who walk in fellowship with Him.

– *Jerry Bridges* –

Justice

jus · tice/ˈdʒʌstɪs/*noun*

1. The upholding of what is just, especially fair treatment and due reward in accordance with honor, standards, or law. **2.** To treat or judge fairly. **3.** Equity, fairness, justness, rightness.

....

Lord, Your justice is eternal.
Ps. 119:142 NLT

The Lord is a God of justice.
Isa. 30:18 NKJV

Surely there is a reward for the righteous;
surely He is God who judges in the earth.
Ps. 58:11 NKJV

....

God is just, and finally justice triumphs.

- Henry Wadsworth Longfellow -

Kindness

kind · ness /ˈkaɪndnəs/ *noun*

1. The practice or quality of being kind. *2.* A kind, considerate or helpful act. *3.* Charity, consideration, generosity, graciousness, understanding, unselfishness.

···

The Lord is filled with kindness.
Ps. 145:17 NLT

Never let loyalty and kindness leave you!
Prov. 3:3 NLT

Therefore, as God's chosen people, holy and dearly loved, clothe yourselves with compassion, kindness, humility, gentleness and patience.
Col. 3:12 NIV

···

A kind heart is a fountain of gladness, making everything in its vicinity freshen into smiles.

– *Washington Irving* –

Knowledge

knowl · edge/ˈnɑːlɪdʒ/*noun*

1. True, justified belief as opposed to opinion. 2. Awareness, consciousness, or familiarity gained by experience or learning. 3. Education, enlightenment, intelligence, scholarship.

....

Give yourselves to disciplined instruction;
open your ears to tested knowledge.
Prov. 23:12 MSG

The wise accumulate knowledge – a true treasure;
know-it-alls talk too much – a sheer waste.
Prov. 10:14 MSG

Drinking from the beautiful chalice of knowledge
is better than adorning oneself with gold and rare gems.
Prov. 20:15 MSG

....

Education is a lifelong journey whose
destination expands as you travel.

- Jim Stovall -

Love

love /lʌv/ *noun*

1. **An intense emotion of affection, warmth, fondness and regard towards a person or a thing.**
2. **God's benevolent attitude towards man and man's attitude of reverent devotion towards God.**
3. **Adoration, admiration, devotion, esteem, tenderness.**

Nothing can separate us from God's love.
Rom. 8:38 NLT

Love is patient, love is kind. It does not envy, it does not boast, it is not proud. It does not dishonor others, it is not self-seeking, it is not easily angered, it keeps no record of wrongs. Love does not delight in evil but rejoices with the truth. It always protects, always trusts, always hopes, always perseveres. Love never fails.
1 Cor. 13:4-8 NIV

People need loving most
when they deserve it the least.

- *John Harrison* -

Loyalty

loy·al·ty/ˈlɔɪəlti/*noun*

1. A strong feeling of support and allegiance.
2. Dependable, dutiful, faithful, staunch, steadfast, unwavering.

. . . .

The Lord protects those who are loyal to Him.
Ps. 31:23 NLT

"If you are faithful in little things,
you will be faithful in large ones."
Luke 16:10 NLT

Don't lose your grip on Love and Loyalty.
Tie them around your neck; carve their initials
on your heart. Earn a reputation for living
well in God's eyes and the eyes of the people.
Prov. 3:3-4 MSG

. . . .

The idea is not that we do work for God,
but that we are so loyal to Him that
He can do His work through us.

- Oswald Chambers -

Marriage

mar · riage /ˈmærɪdʒ/ *noun*

1. The formal union of a man and a woman, typically as recognized by law and ordained by God, by which they become husband and wife. **2.** Matrimony, wedlock, union.

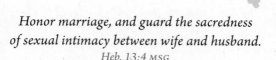

Honor marriage, and guard the sacredness
of sexual intimacy between wife and husband.
Heb. 13:4 MSG

A man leaves his father and mother and is
joined to his wife, and the two are united into one.
Eph. 5:31 NLT

Let the husband render to his wife the affection
due her, and likewise also the wife to her husband.
1 Cor. 7:3 NKJV

Be the mate God designed you to be.

– Anthony T. Evans –

Memories

mem · o · ries /'meməris/ *noun*

1. The ability of the mind to store and recall past sensations, thoughts, knowledge, experiences.
2. Memento, recollection, remembrance, reminder, token, souvenir.

....

I will remember the works of the Lord;
surely I will remember Your wonders of old.
Ps. 77:11 NKJV

I remember the days of old. I ponder all Your
great works and think about what You have done.
Ps. 143:5 NLT

"I, even I, am He who blots out your transgressions
for My own sake; and I will not remember your sins."
Isa. 43:25 NKJV

....

Live an honorable life. Then when you get older and
think back, you'll be able to enjoy it a second time.

– Anonymous –

Mercy

mer · cy /'mɜːrsi/ *noun*

1. Compassionate treatment of or attitude towards an offender, adversary, who is in one's power or care. 2. God's act of forgiving sinful yet repentant people. 3. Benevolence, clemency, compassion, forbearance, forgiveness, humanity.

....

The Lord's mercy endures forever.
2 Chron. 7:3 NKJV

You, God, delight to show mercy.
Mic. 7:18 NIV

"The God of compassion and mercy! I am slow to anger and filled with unfailing love and faithfulness. I forgive iniquity, rebellion, and sin."
Exod. 34:6-7 NLT

....

Among the attributes of God, although they are all equal, mercy shines with even more brilliance than justice.

- *Miguel de Cervantes* -

Obedience

o · be · di · ence/əˈbiːdiəns/**noun**

1. The act or an instance of obeying; dutiful or submissive behavior. **2.** Acquiescence, allegiance, compliance, submission.

....

Once made perfect, He [Jesus] became the source of eternal salvation for all who obey Him.
Heb. 5:9 NIV

"Therefore whoever hears these sayings of Mine, and does them, I will liken him to a wise man who built his house on the rock: and the rain descended, the floods came, and the winds blew and beat on that house; and it did not fall, for it was founded on the rock."
Matt. 7:24-25 NKJV

"Obey My laws and live by My decrees. I am your God."
Lev. 18:1 MSG

....

God desires the least degree of obedience and submissiveness more than all those services you think of rendering Him.

– *John of the Cross* –

Optimism

op · ti · mism/ˈɑːptɪmɪzəm/*noun*

1. The tendency to expect the best and see the best in all things. *2.* The belief that good must ultimately prevail over evil in the universe. *3.* Cheerfulness, confidence, hopefulness, looking on the bright side, trust.

....

Look forward to the gracious salvation that will come to you when Jesus Christ is revealed to the world.
1 Pet. 1:13 NLT

We don't yet see things clearly. We're squinting in a fog, peering through a mist. But it won't be long before the weather clears and the sun shines bright! We'll see it all then, see it all as clearly as God sees us, knowing Him directly just as He knows us!
1 Cor. 13:12 MSG

Now to Him who can keep you on your feet, standing tall in His bright presence, fresh and celebrating – to our one God, our only Savior, through Jesus Christ be glory, majesty, strength, and rule before all time, and now, and to the end of all time. Yes.
Jude 24 MSG

....

One can never consent to creep when one feels an impulse to soar.

- *Helen Keller* -

Patience

pa · tience /ˈpeɪʃns/ ***noun***

1. Tolerant and even-tempered perseverance.
2. The capacity for calmly enduring pain,
delay, trouble, suffering. **3.** Forbearance,
determination, long-suffering, persistence,
perseverance, resolution.

···

I waited patiently for the Lord to help me,
and He turned to me and heard my cry.
Ps. 40:1 NLT

The Lord is patient with you, not wanting anyone
to perish, but everyone to come to repentance.
2 Pet. 3:9 NIV

Patient endurance is what you need now,
so that you will continue to do God's will.
Then you will receive all that He has promised.
Heb. 10:36 NLT

···

Patient waiting is often the
highest way of doing God's will.

- Jeremy Collier -

Peace

peace/piːs/*noun*

1. **A state of stillness, silence or serenity.** *2.* **In a state of harmony or friendship.** *3.* **Absence of mental and emotional anxiety.** *4.* **Calm, placid, quiet, restful, untroubled.**

. . . .

In peace I will lie down and sleep,
for You alone, O Lord, will keep me safe.
Ps. 4:8 NLT

The Lord will bless His people with peace.
Ps. 29:11 NKJV

The peace of God, which transcends
all understanding, will guard your
hearts and your minds in Christ Jesus.
Phil. 4:7 NIV

. . . .

Christ alone can bring lasting peace –
peace with God – peace among men
and nations – and peace within our hearts.

- Billy Graham -

Perseverance

per · se · ver · ance /ˌpɜːrsəˈvɪrəns/ ***noun***

1. Steady persistence in adhering to a course of action, a belief, or a purpose. **2.** Continued steady belief or efforts, withstanding discouragement or difficulty; persistence. **3.** Determined, resolved, resolute, steadfast.

···

You need to persevere so that when you have done the will of God, you will receive what He has promised.
Heb. 10:36 NIV

Therefore, since we are surrounded by such a great cloud of witnesses, let us throw off everything that hinders and the sin that so easily entangles. And let us run with perseverance the race marked out for us.
Heb. 12:1 NIV

Blessed is the one who perseveres under trial because, having stood the test, that person will receive the crown of life that the Lord has promised to those who love Him.
James 1:12 NIV

···

Aim at heaven and you will get earth thrown in.
Aim at earth and you get neither.

- C. S. Lewis -

Prayer

prayer/prer/*noun*

1. A solemn request for help or expression of thanks addressed to God. *2.* The act of making a reverent petition to God. *3.* The very essence of a faith relationship with God. *4.* Adoration, two-way communication, glorification, praise, thanksgiving, worship.

....

Don't fret or worry. Instead of worrying, pray.
Let petitions and praises shape your worries
into prayers, letting God know your concerns.
Phil. 4:6 MSG

The Lord is near to all who call upon Him,
to all who call upon Him in truth.
Ps. 145:18 NKJV

Don't quit in hard times; pray all the harder.
Rom. 12:12 MSG

....

Prayer is not monologue, but dialogue. God's voice in response to mine is its most essential part.

- Andrew Murray -

Promises

prom·ises/'prɑːmɪses/*noun*

1. A declaration assuring that one will or will not do something; a vow. *2.* Indication of something favorable to come; expectation. *3.* To commit oneself by a promise to do or give. *4.* Assurance, declaration, guarantee, pledge, word of honor.

. . . .

Let us hold tightly without wavering to the hope we affirm, for God can be trusted to keep His promise.
Heb. 10:23 NLT

God has given both His promise and His oath. These two things are unchangeable because it is impossible for God to lie.
Heb. 6:18 NLT

Don't trap yourself by making a rash promise to God and only later counting the cost.
Prov. 20:25 NLT

. . . .

Let God's promises shine on your problems.

– Corrie ten Boom –

Protection

pro · tec · tion/prə'tekʃn/*noun*

....

1. The act of protecting. *2.* The condition of being protected. *3.* One who protects. *4.* Buffer, guard, refuge, safeguard, sanctuary, shelter, shield.

....

God's a safe-house for the battered, a sanctuary during bad times. The moment you arrive, you relax; you're never sorry you knocked.
Ps. 9:9-10 MSG

God guards you from every evil, He guards your very life. He guards you when you leave and when you return, He guards you now, He guards you always.
Ps. 121:7-8 MSG

My God is my rock, in whom I find protection.
2 Sam. 22:3 NLT

....

The safest place in all the world is in the will of God, and the safest protection in all the world is the name of God.

– *Warren Wiersbe* –

Provision

pro · vi · sion /prəˈvɪʒn/ *noun*

1. The action of providing something for use.
2. Something provided. **3.** Giving, supplying,
sustenance.

....

*He who supplies seed to the sower and bread for
food will also supply and increase your store of seed
and will enlarge the harvest of your righteousness.*
2 Cor. 9:10 NIV

*The Lord has given food to those who fear Him;
He will ever be mindful of His covenant.*
Ps. 111:5 NKJV

*My God shall supply all your need
according to His riches in glory by Christ Jesus.*
Phil. 4:19 NKJV

....

Abundance isn't God's provision for
me to live in luxury, but His provision
for me to help others to live.

- Randy Alcorn -

Purpose

pur · pose /ˈpɜːrpəs/ *noun*

1. The reason for which something is done or created or for which something exists. *2.* Fixed intention in doing something; determination. *3.* Aim, design, function, meaning, sense.

....

The Lord will perfect that which concerns me;
Your mercy, O Lord, endures forever;
do not forsake the works of Your hands.
Ps. 138:8 NKJV

One thing I do, forgetting those things which
are behind and reaching forward to those things
which are ahead, I press toward the goal for the
prize of the upward call of God in Christ Jesus.
Phil. 3:13-14 NKJV

I am certain that God, who began the good
work within you, will continue His work until it is
finally finished on the day when Christ Jesus returns.
Phil. 1:6 NLT

....

In Christ alone, and His payment of the penalty
for our sins upon the Cross, we find reconciliation
to God and ultimate meaning and purpose.

– Dave Hunt –

Reassurance

re · as · sur · ance /ˌriːəˈʃʊrəns/ ***noun***

1. **The action of removing someone's doubts or fears. 2. A statement or comment that removes someone's doubts or fears. 3. Comfort, encourage, inspire hope, set someone's mind at rest.**

The Spirit is God's guarantee that He will give us the inheritance He promised and that He has purchased us to be His own people.
Eph. 1:14 NLT

For He Himself has said, "I will never leave you nor forsake you."
Heb. 13:5 NKJV

God reminds us, I heard your call in the nick of time; the day you needed Me, I was there to help.
2 Cor. 6:2 MSG

Blessed assurance, Jesus is mine.
O what a foretaste of glory divine!

- Fanny Crosby -

Refuge

ref·uge/'refjuːdʒ/**noun**

1. A condition of being safe or sheltered from pursuit, danger, or trouble. 2. Something providing such shelter. 3. Asylum, haven, harbor, retreat, sanctuary.

....

I will sing of Your strength, in the morning I will sing of Your love; for You are my fortress, my refuge in times of trouble.
Ps. 59:16 NIV

God is a safe place to hide, ready to help when we need Him. We stand fearless at the cliff-edge of doom, courageous in seastorm and earthquake.
Ps. 46:1 MSG

The Lord is my rock and my fortress and my deliverer; my God, my strength, in whom I will trust; my shield and the horn of my salvation, my stronghold.
Ps. 18:2 NKJV

....

Where does your security lie? Is God your refuge, your hiding place, your stronghold, your shepherd, your counselor, your friend, your redeemer, your savior, your guide? If He is, you don't need to search any further for security.

– *Elizabeth Elliot* –

Relationship

re·la·tion·ship/rɪˈleɪʃnʃɪp/*noun*

1. The mutual dealings, connections, or feelings that exist between two people or parties. 2. Association, affiliation, connection, bond, link, tie.

··

In your relationships with one another,
have the same mindset as Christ Jesus.
Phil. 2:5 NIV

Anyone who remains in the teaching of Christ
has a relationship with both the Father and the Son.
2 John 1:9 NLT

You must worship no other gods, for the Lord,
whose very name is Jealous, is a God who
is jealous about His relationship with you.
Exod. 34:14 NLT

··

If you want people to be glad to meet you, you
must be glad to meet them — and show it.

- *Johann Wolfgang von Goethe* -

Renewal

re · new · al /rɪˈnuːəl/ *noun*

1. The act of renewing or the state of having been renewed. 2. Something renewed. 3. Regenerate, rejuvenate, refresh, revive, save, salvage, redeem.

....

Create in me a clean heart, O God,
and renew a steadfast spirit within me.
Ps. 51:10 NIV

Therefore we do not lose heart.
Though outwardly we are wasting away,
yet inwardly we are being renewed day by day.
2 Cor. 4:16 NIV

He wraps you in goodness – beauty eternal. He renews
your youth – you're always young in His presence.
Ps. 103:5 MSG

....

It is good to renew ourselves by
closely examining the state of our souls;
for nothing tends more to the full assurance
of faith, than to keep ourselves by this means
in humility, and the exercise of all good works.

– John Wesley –

Reputation

rep·u·ta·tion /ˌrepjuˈteɪʃn/ *noun*

1. The estimation in which a person or thing is generally held; opinion **2.** A high opinion generally held about a person or thing; esteem. **3.** Name, repute, standing, stature.

....

Choose a good reputation over great riches;
being held in high esteem is better than silver or gold.
Prov. 22:1 NLT

A good reputation is more valuable than costly perfume.
Eccles. 7:1 NLT

In Joppa there was a disciple named Tabitha;
she was always doing good and helping the poor.
Acts 9:36 NIV

....

If I take care of my character,
my reputation will take care of itself.

- Dwight L. Moody -

Respect

re · spect /ri'spekt/ *noun*

1. To show consideration for; treat courteously or kindly. **2.** Willingness to show consideration or appreciation. **3.** Consider, esteem, honor, value, understand.

·······························

Show proper respect to everyone,
love the family of believers, fear God.
1 Pet. 2:17 NIV

A person with good sense is respected.
Prov. 13:15 NLT

"Stand up in the presence of the elderly,
and show respect for the aged."
Lev. 19:32 NLT

·······························

When respect is earned, it will
first be evident on the inside.

– *Woodrow Kroll* –

Responsibility

re · spon · si · bil · i · ty /rɪˌspɑːnsəˈbɪləti/ ***noun***

1. The state, quality, or fact of being responsible.
2. Something for which one is responsible; a
duty, obligation, or burden. ***3.*** Accountability,
answerability, dependability, reliability,
trustworthiness.

....

We are each responsible for our own conduct.
Gal. 6:5 NLT

*"Well done, my good and faithful servant.
You have been faithful in handling this small amount,
so now I will give you many more responsibilities."*
Matt. 25:21 NLT

*Be a good citizen. All governments are under God.
Insofar as there is peace and order, it's God's order.
So live responsibly as a citizen.*
Rom. 13:1 MSG

....

Do your duty, and leave the rest to God.
- Richard Cecil -

Rest

rest/rest/*noun*

1. Peace, ease, or refreshment resulting from sleep or the cessation of an activity. *2.* Sleep or quiet relaxation. *3.* Mental or emotional tranquility. *4.* Breather, peace, respite, relaxation, sleep, quiet.

. . . .

He who dwells in the secret place of the Most High shall abide under the shadow of the Almighty.
Ps. 91:1 NKJV

"Come to Me, all you who labor and are heavy laden, and I will give you rest."
Matt. 11:28 NKJV

Therefore my heart is glad, and my glory rejoices; my flesh also will rest in hope.
Ps. 16:9 NKJV

. . . .

You have created us for Yourself, and our heart cannot be stilled until it finds its rest in You.

- St. Augustine -

Salvation

sal · va · tion /sæl'veɪʃn/ *noun*

1. Deliverance from the consequences of sin through the death and resurrection of Jesus Christ. *2.* Resulting in rebirth, renewal and eternal life. *3.* Atonement, freedom, justification, redemption, sanctification.

....

For God so loved the world that He gave His only begotten Son, that whoever believes in Him should not perish but have everlasting life.
John 3:16 NKJV

"Though your sins are like scarlet, they shall be as white as snow; though they are red like crimson, they shall be as wool."
Isa. 1:18 NKJV

For the wages of sin is death, but the gift of God is eternal life in Christ Jesus our Lord.
Rom. 6:23 NKJV

....

He who created us without our help will not save us without our consent.

- St. Augustine -

Security

se·cu·ri·ty/səˈkjʊrəti/*noun*

1. **Freedom from risk or danger.** *2.* **Freedom from doubt, anxiety, or fear; confidence.** *3.* **Something that gives or assures safety.** *4.* **Care, freedom from harm, protection, safety.**

....

The Lord is your security. He will keep your foot from being caught in a trap.
Prov. 3:26 NLT

The Lord is my light and my salvation – whom shall I fear? The Lord is the stronghold of my life – of whom shall I be afraid?
Ps. 27:1 NIV

He has identified us as His own by placing the Holy Spirit in our hearts as the first installment that guarantees everything He has promised us.
2 Cor. 1:22 NLT

....

In His love He clothes us, enfolds us and embraces; that tender love completely surrounds us, never to leave us

– Julian of Norwich –

Self-control

self-con · trol/self-kən'troʊl/*noun*

1. Control of one's emotions, desires, or actions by one's own will. **2.** Composure, forbearance, self-discipline, self-possession, temperance, will-power.

....

Put on the Lord Jesus Christ, and make no provision for the flesh, to fulfill its lusts.
Rom. 13:14 NKJV

If anyone among you thinks he is religious, and does not bridle his tongue but deceives his own heart, this one's religion is useless.
James 1:26 NKJV

God has not given us a spirit of fear and timidity, but of power, love, and self-discipline.
2 Tim. 1:7 NLT

....

Self-control is the exercise of inner strength under the direction of sound judgment that enables us to do, think, and say the things that are pleasing to God.

- *Jerry Bridges* -

Self-worth

self-worth/self–wɜːrθ/*noun*

1. Accepting who you are in Christ as a cherished, loved and forgiven child of God.
2. Dignity, self-esteem, self-respect.

....

God pays even greater attention to you, down to the last detail – even numbering the hairs on your head!
Luke 12:7 MSG

We are transfigured much like the Messiah, our lives gradually becoming brighter and more beautiful as God enters our lives and we become like Him.
2 Cor. 3:18 MSG

I praise You because I am fearfully and wonderfully made; Your works are wonderful, I know that full well.
Ps. 139:14 NIV

....

To encounter Christ is to touch reality and experience transcendence. He gives us a sense of self-worth or personal significance, because He assures us of God's love for us. He sets us free from guilt because He died for us and from paralyzing fear because He reigns.

- *John Stott* -

Service

ser · vice /ˈsɜːrvɪs /*noun*

1. **An act of assistance or benefit; a favor: 2.** The offering of time, money and energy in active devotion to God and the church. **3.** Assistance, effort, help, support, usefulness.

....

There are different kinds of service, but we serve the same Lord. God works in different ways, but it is the same God who does the work in all of us.
1 Cor. 12:5-6 NLT

"Whoever wants to become great among you must be your servant, and whoever wants to be first must be your slave."
Matt. 20:26-27 NIV

Those who have served well gain an excellent standing and great assurance in their faith in Christ Jesus.
1 Tim. 3:13 NIV

....

Life is an exciting business, and it is most exciting when it is lived for others.

– Helen Keller –

Strength

strength /streŋθ/ *noun*

1. The ability to maintain a moral or intellectual position firmly. *2.* A source of power or force. *3.* One that is regarded as the embodiment of protective or supportive power; a support or mainstay. *4.* Anchor, forte, support.

....

I pray that you will understand the incredible greatness of God's power for us who believe Him.
Eph. 1:19 NLT

He gives power to the weak, and to those who have no might He increases strength.
Isa. 40:29 NKJV

Those who wait on the Lord shall renew their strength; they shall mount up with wings like eagles, they shall run and not be weary, they shall walk and not faint.
Isa. 40:31 NKJV

....

In all my perplexities and distresses, the Bible has never failed to give me light and strength.

- Robert E. Lee -

Success

suc·cess /sək'ses/ *noun*

1. The achievement of something desired, planned, or attempted. *2.* An action or performance that is characterized by success. *3.* A person or thing that is successful. *4.* Achievement, attainment, prosperity, triumph, victory.

....

Commit your actions to the Lord,
and your plans will succeed.
Prov. 16:3 NLT

Therefore, my beloved brethren, be steadfast,
immovable, always abounding in the work of the Lord,
knowing that your labor is not in vain in the Lord.
1 Cor. 15:58 NKJV

Through God we will do valiantly, for it
is He who shall tread down our enemies.
Ps. 60:12 NKJV

....

The only place where success comes
before work is in the dictionary.

– Vidal Sassoon –

Thanksgiving

thanks · giv · ing /ˌθæŋksˈgɪvɪŋ/ *noun*

1. An act of giving thanks; an expression of gratitude, especially to God. 2. Appreciation, blessing, celebration, grace, gratitude, thankfulness.

....

Oh, give thanks to the Lord, for He is good!
For His mercy endures forever.
1 Chron. 16:34 NKJV

Thank God! He gives us victory over sin
and death through our Lord Jesus Christ.
1 Cor. 15:57 NLT

Enter into His gates with thanksgiving,
and into His courts with praise.
Be thankful to Him, and bless His name.
Ps. 100:4 NKJV

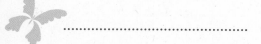

....

We would worry less if we praised more. Thanksgiving is the enemy of discontent and dissatisfaction.

– Harry Ironside –

Thoughts

thoughts /θɔːts/ *noun*

1. An idea or opinion produced by thinking or occurring suddenly in the mind. *2.* An idea or mental picture, imagined and contemplated. *3.* Contemplation, deliberation, meditation, musings reflection.

....

For He will bring our darkest secrets to light and will reveal our private motives. Then God will give to each one whatever praise is due.
Ps. 4:5 NLT

Finally, brothers and sisters, whatever is true, whatever is noble, whatever is right, whatever is pure, whatever is lovely, whatever is admirable – if anything is excellent or praiseworthy – think about such things.
Phil. 4:8 NIV

How precious are Your thoughts about me, O God. They cannot be numbered!
Ps. 139:17 NLT

....

Without doubt the mightiest thought the mind can entertain is the thought of God.

– A. W. Tozer –

Time

time /taɪm/ *noun*

1. A nonspatial continuum in which events occur in apparently irreversible succession from the past through the present to the future. *2.* Period designated for a given activity *3.* Continuation of all existence, duration, interval, span of time, season.

....

To everything there is a season,
a time for every purpose under heaven.
Eccles. 3:1 NKJV

Humble yourselves under the mighty power of God,
and at the right time He will lift you up in honor.
1 Pet. 5:6 NLT

You are my God! Hour by hour
I place my days in Your hand.
Ps. 31:14-15 MSG

....

No time is so well spent in every day as
that which we spend upon our knees.

- *J. C. Ryle* -

Trust

trust/trʌst/**noun**

1. **Firm reliance on the integrity, ability, or character of a person or thing.** *2.* **One in which confidence is placed.** *3.* **Belief, confidence, conviction, dependence, faith.**

I trust in You for salvation, O Lord!
Gen. 49:18 NLT

Those who know Your name trust in You, for You, Lord, have never forsaken those who seek You.
Ps. 9:10 NIV

I trust in You, Lord; I say, "You are my God."
Ps. 31:14 NIV

Trust the past to God's mercy, the present to God's love and the future to God's providence.

- St. Augustine -

Truth

truth/tru:θ/*noun*

1. **The quality of being true, genuine, actual, or factual.** *2.* **Conformity to fact or actuality.** *3.* **Authenticity, exactness, fact, proven principle, reality.**

....

Jesus said to him, "I am the way, the truth, and the life. No one comes to the Father except through Me."
John 14:6 NKJV

Then Jesus turned to the Jews who had claimed to believe in Him. "If you stick with this, living out what I tell you, you are My disciples for sure. Then you will experience for yourselves the truth, and the truth will free you."
John 8:31 MSG

All Scripture is inspired by God and is useful to teach us what is true and to make us realize what is wrong in our lives. It corrects us when we are wrong and teaches us to do what is right.
2 Tim. 3:16 NLT

....

The gospel is not speculation but fact. It is truth, because it is the record of a Person who is the Truth.

- *Alexander MacLaren* -

Understanding

un · der · stand · ing /ˌʌndər'stændɪŋ/ *noun*

1. The quality or condition of one who understands; comprehension. *2.* A disposition to appreciate or share the feelings and thoughts of others; sympathy. *3.* Discernment, empathy, good sense, insight, perception.

....

The Lord searches all hearts and
understands all the intent of the thoughts.
If you seek Him, He will be found by you.
1 Chron. 28:9 NKJV

May the Lord lead your hearts into a full
understanding and expression of the love of God
and the patient endurance that comes from Christ.
2 Thess. 3:5 NLT

Great is our Lord, and mighty in power;
His understanding is infinite.
Ps. 147:5 NKJV

....

Forgive, forget. Bear with the faults
of others as you would have them bear
with yours. Be patient and understanding.
Life is too short to be vengeful or malicious.

– Phillips Brooks –

Uniqueness

u · nique · ness /juˈniːknəs/ *noun*

1. Being the only one of its kind. 2. Without an equal or equivalent. 3. Distinctive, incomparable, matchless, unequalled, unparalleled, unrivalled.

....

I paid a huge price for you: That's how much you mean to Me! That's how much I love you! I'd sell off the whole world to get you back, trade the creation just for you.
Isa. 43:4 MSG

You have been set apart as holy to the Lord your God, and He has chosen you from all the nations of the earth to be His own special treasure.
Deut. 14:2 NLT

There's no one like her on earth, never has been, never will be. She's a woman beyond compare. My dove is perfection, pure and innocent as the day she was born, and cradled in joy by her mother.
Song of Solomon 6:8 MSG

....

God loves each of us as if there were only one of us.

- St. Augustine -

Virtue

vir · tue/'vɜːrtʃuː/*noun*

1. Moral excellence and righteousness.
2. An example or kind of moral excellence.
3. Goodness, honesty, honor, integrity,
righteousness.

....

"So in everything, do to others what
you would have them do to you, for
this sums up the Law and the Prophets."
Matt. 7:12 NIV

He's already made it plain how to live, what to do,
what God is looking for in men and women. It's quite
simple: Do what is fair and just to your neighbor,
be compassionate and loyal in your love, and don't
take yourself too seriously – take God seriously.
Mic. 6:8 MSG

Treat everyone you meet with dignity. Love your
spiritual family. Revere God. Respect the government.
1 Pet. 2:17 MSG

....

What the world calls virtue is a name and a dream
without Christ. The foundation of all human
excellence must be laid deep in the blood of the
Redeemer's cross and in the power of His resurrection.

– Frederick Robertson –

Wealth

wealth /welθ/ *noun*

1. **An abundance of valuable material possessions or resources. 2. The state of being rich; affluence. 3. A great amount; a profusion. 4. Fortune, resources, riches.**

. . . .

Command those who are rich in this present age not to be haughty, nor to trust in uncertain riches but in the living God, who gives us richly all things to enjoy.
1 Tim. 6:17 NKJV

God will generously provide all you need. Then you will always have everything you need and plenty left over to share with others.
2 Cor. 9:8 NLT

Honor the Lord with your wealth and with the best part of everything you produce. Then He will fill your barns with grain, and your vats will overflow with good wine.
Prov. 3:9-10 NIV

. . . .

If you want to feel rich, just count all
the things you have that money can't buy.

– Anonymous –

Wisdom

wis · dom /ˈwɪzdəm/ *noun*

1. The ability to discern or judge what is true, right, or lasting; insight. *2.* Common sense; good judgment. *3.* A wise outlook, plan, or course of action. *4.* Discernment, good judgment, intelligence, understanding.

···

The Lord gives wisdom; from His mouth come knowledge and understanding.
Prov. 2:6 NKJV

Fear of the Lord is the foundation of true wisdom. All who obey His commandments will grow in wisdom.
Ps. 111:10 NLT

If any of you lacks wisdom, let him ask of God, who gives to all liberally and without reproach, and it will be given to him.
James 1:5 NKJV

···

Wisdom is the right use of knowledge. To know is not to be wise. Many men know a great deal, and are all the greater fools for it. There is no fool so great a fool as a knowing fool. But to know how to use knowledge is to have wisdom.

- Charles. H. Spurgeon -

Womanhood

wom · an · hood /ˈwʊmənhʊd/ *noun*

1. The state or time of being a woman. **2.** The composite of qualities thought to be appropriate to or representative of women. **3.** Caregiver, listener, mother, nurturer, provider, sister, wife.

···

Charm is deceitful and beauty is passing, but a woman who fears the Lord, she shall be praised. Give her of the fruit of her hands, and let her own works praise her in the gates.
Prov. 31:30-31 NKJV

A gracious woman gains respect.
Prov. 11:16 NLT

Strength and honor are her clothing; she shall rejoice in time to come. She opens her mouth with wisdom, and on her tongue is the law of kindness. She watches over the ways of her household, and does not eat the bread of idleness.
Prov. 31:25-27 NKJV

···

Next to God we are indebted to women, first for life itself, and then for making it worth having.

– Christian Boveé –

Worship

wor · ship /ˈwɜːrʃɪp/ *noun*

1. The reverent love and devotion accorded to God by believers. **2.** The prayers, praise and other forms by which this love is expressed. **3.** Ardent devotion, adoration, exalt, extol, glorify, praise, revere, reverence, venerate.

....

Great is the Lord! He is most worthy of praise!
He is to be feared above all gods.
Ps. 96:4 NLT

Therefore, since we are receiving a kingdom
that cannot be shaken, let us be thankful, and
so worship God acceptably with reverence and awe.
Heb. 12:28 NIV

Worship the Lord with gladness;
come before Him with joyful songs.
Ps. 100:2 NIV

....

God is not moved or impressed with our worship
until our hearts are moved and impressed by Him.

– Kelly Sparks –

Worthiness

wor · thi · ness /ˈwɜːrðinəs/ *noun*

1. Having worth, merit, or value; useful or valuable. *2.* Honorable; admirable. *3.* Having sufficient worth; deserving.

....

"I knew you before I formed you in your mother's womb. Before you were born I set you apart."
Jer. 1:5 NLT

Behold what manner of love the Father has bestowed on us, that we should be called children of God!
1 John 3:1 NKJV

Great is the Lord and most worthy of praise; His greatness no one can fathom.
Ps. 145:3 NIV

....

Worship is the specific act of ascribing to God the glory, majesty, honor, and worthiness which are His.

- Jerry Bridges -

The Word of God on Words

....

A word aptly spoken is like
apples of gold in settings of silver.
Prov. 25:11 NIV

Let my words and my thoughts
be pleasing to you, Lord.
Ps. 19:14 CEV

The words of the wise bring them praise.
Eccles. 10:12 NCV

Saying the right word at the
right time is so pleasing.
Prov. 15:23 NCV

....

The Word of God on Words

....

Words kill, words give life; they're
either poison or fruit – you choose.
Prov. 18:21 MSG

Wise words bring many benefits.
Prov. 12:14 NLT

Gentle words are a tree of life.
Prov. 15:4 NLT

Kind words are like honey –
sweet to the soul and healthy to the body.
Prov. 16:24 NLT

....

Words That Have Touched My Heart ...

_____

_____

_____

_____

_____

_____

_____

_____

_____

_____

_____